OC 28 02	DATE DUE		
MR 28 '03			

LOOKING INTO THE PAST:
PEOPLE, PLACES, AND CUSTOMS

Egyptian Kings and Queens and Classical Deities

by

Dwayne E. Pickels

Chelsea House Publishers

CHELSEA HOUSE PUBLISHERS
Editor-in-Chief Stephen Reginald
Managing Editor James D. Gallagher
Production Manager Pamela Loos
Art Director Sara Davis
Picture Editor Judy Hasday
Senior Production Editor Lisa Chippendale
Designer Takeshi Takahashi

3 5 7 9 8 6 4

Library of Congress Cataloging-in-Publication Data

Pickels, Dwayne E.
Egyptian kings and queens and classical deities / by Dwayne
E. Pickels.

p. cm. — (Looking into the Past: people, places, and cus-
toms)
Includes bibliographical references and index.
Summary: Introduces a dozen kings and queens of ancient
Egypt and relates the often amazing exploits of other figures
from the classical age of Greek and Roman mythology.

ISBN 0-7910-4677-X

1. Pharaohs—Juvenile literature. 2. Queens—Egypt—Juvenile
literature. 3. Egypt—History—To 640 A.D.—Juvenile litera-
ture. 4. Mythology, Greek—Juvenile literature. 5. Mythology,
Roman—Juvenile literature. [1. Egypt—History—To 640
A.D. 2. Mythology, Greek. 3. Mythology, Roman. 4. Kings,
Queens, rulers, etc.] I. Title. II. Series: Looking into the past.
DT83.A2P5   1997
930'.3—dc21   97-25504
                                              CIP
                                              AC

CONTENTS

CULTURE, CUSTOMS, AND RITUALS

The important moments of our lives—from birth through puberty, aging, and death—are made more meaningful by culture, customs, and rituals. But what is culture? The word *culture,* broadly defined, includes the way of life of an entire society. This encompasses customs, rituals, codes of manners, dress, languages, norms of behavior, and systems of beliefs. Individuals are both acted on by and react to a culture—and so generate new cultural forms and customs.

What is custom? Custom refers to accepted social practices that separate one cultural group from another. Every culture contains basic customs, often known as rites of transition or passage. These rites, or ceremonies, occur at different stages of life, from birth to death, and are sometimes religious in nature. In all cultures of the world today, a new baby is greeted and welcomed into its family through ceremony. Some ceremonies, such as the bar mitzvah, a religious initiation for teenage Jewish boys, mark the transition from childhood to adulthood. Marriage also is usually celebrated by a ritual of some sort. Death is another rite of transition. All known cultures contain beliefs about life after death, and all observe funeral rites and mourning customs.

What is a ritual? What is a rite? These terms are used interchangeably to describe a ceremony associated with a custom. The English ritual of shaking hands in greeting, for example, has become part of that culture. The washing of one's hands could be considered a ritual which helps a person achieve an accepted level of cleanliness—a requirement of the cultural beliefs that person holds.

The books in this series, *Looking into the Past: People,*

Places, and Customs, explore many of the most interesting rituals of different cultures through time. For example, did you know that in the year A.D. 1075 William the Conqueror ordered that a "Couvre feu" bell be rung at sunset in each town and city of England, as a signal to put out all fires? Because homes were made of wood and had thatched roofs, the bell served as a precaution against house fires. Today, this custom is no longer observed as it was 900 years ago, but the modern word *curfew* derives from its practice.

Another ritual that dates from centuries long past is the Japanese Samurai Festival. This colorful celebration commemorates the feats of the ancient samurai warriors who ruled the country hundreds of years ago. Japanese citizens dress in costumes, and direct descendants of warriors wear samurai swords during the festival. The making of these swords actually is a separate religious rite in itself.

Different cultures develop different customs. For example, people of different nations have developed various interesting ways to greet each other. In China 100 years ago, the ordinary salutation was a ceremonious, but not deep, bow, with the greeting "Kin t'ien ni hao ma?" (Are you well today?). During the same era, citizens of the Indian Ocean island nation Ceylon (now called Sri Lanka) greeted each other by placing their palms together with the fingers extended. When greeting a person of higher social rank, the hands were held in front of the forehead and the head was inclined.

Some symbols and rituals rooted in ancient beliefs are common to several cultures. For example, in China, Japan, and many of the countries of the East, a tortoise is a symbol of protection from black magic, while fish have represented fertility, new life, and prosperity since the beginnings of human civilization. Other ancient fertility symbols have been incorporated into religions we still practice today, and so these ancient beliefs remain a part of our civilization. A more recent belief, the legend of Santa Claus, is the story of a kind benefactor who brings gifts to the good children of the world. This story appears in the lore of nearly every nation. Each country developed its own variation on the legend and each celebrates Santa's arrival in a different way.

New rituals are being created all the time. On April 21, 1997, for example, the cremated remains of 24 people were launched into orbit around Earth on a Pegasus rocket. Included among the group whose ashes now head toward their "final frontier" are Gene Roddenberry, creator of the television series *Star Trek,* and Timothy Leary, a countercultural icon of the 1960s. Each person's remains were placed in a separate aluminum capsule engraved with the person's name and a commemorative phrase. The remains will orbit the Earth every 90 minutes for two to ten years. When the rocket does re-enter Earth's atmosphere, it will burn up with a great burst of light. This first-time ritual could become an accepted rite of passage, a custom in our culture that would supplant the current ceremonies marking the transition between life and death.

Curiosity about different customs, rites, and rituals dates back to the mercantile Greeks of classical times. Herodotus (484–425 B.C.), known as the "Father of History," described Egyptian culture. The Roman historian Tacitus (A.D. 55–117) similarly wrote a lengthy account about the customs of the "modern" European barbarians. From the Greeks to Marco Polo, from Columbus to the Pacific voyages of Captain James Cook, cultural differences have fascinated the literate world. The books in the *Looking into the Past* series collect the most interesting customs from many cultures of the past and explain their origins, meanings, and relationship to the present day.

In the future, space travel may very well provide the impetus for new cultures, customs, and rituals, which will in turn enthrall and interest the peoples of future millennia.

Fred L. Israel
The City College of the City University of New York

CONTRIBUTORS

Senior Consulting Editor FRED L. ISRAEL is an award-winning historian. He received the Scribe's Award from the American Bar Association for his work on the Chelsea House series *The Justices of the United States Supreme Court.* A specialist in early American history, he was general editor for Chelsea's *1897 Sears Roebuck Catalog.* Dr. Israel has also worked in association with Dr. Arthur M. Schlesinger, jr. on many projects, including *The History of U.S. Presidential Elections* and *The History of U.S. Political Parties.* They are currently working together on the Chelsea House series *The World 100 Years Ago,* which looks at the traditions, customs, and cultures of many nations at the turn of the century.

DWAYNE E. PICKELS is an award-winning reporter with the *Greensburg (Pa.) Tribune-Review.* A Magna Cum Laude graduate of the University of Pittsburgh, where he cofounded the literary magazine *Pendulum,* Dwayne won a Pennsylvania Newspaper Publishers' Association (PNPA) Keystone Press Award in 1992. He currently resides in Scottdale, Pa., with his wife, Mary, and their daughter, Kaidia Leigh. In his free time, he is currently immersed in a number of literary pursuits—which include a novel based on Celtic myth and legend. In addition to writing, Dwayne enjoys outdoor excursions, including bird watching, hiking, photography, and target shooting . . . along with typically futile attempts at fishing.

Overview

The Deities of Antiquity

From the shores of the Nile to the heights of Mount Olympus, the wisdom of the ages comes to us from many sources. Few of us can conjure images of ancient Egypt in our minds without envisioning great pyramids and glittering, gold-filled burial tombs. But these colossal and ornate trappings of the long dead are only monuments and clues to the lives of the people who left them—Rameses, Amenophis, Cleopatra. And when we gaze up into the vast night sky at the planets that journey with us around the sun and trace the stellar patterns that dance around the North Star, we recall the grand myths that gave these heavenly bodies and constellations their legendary names—Venus and Mars, Jupiter and Andromeda.

Despite all the technological marvels of these modern times, and the knowledge they've brought closer to perfection, we will always remain indebted to these early civilizations. For it was the Greeks, Romans, and Egyptians, and others like them, who gave shape to the very universe with their wondrous gods and goddesses. For it was through them that our ancestors began to ponder and understand the secret workings of themselves and the world around them. And it was their great kings and queens who forged the mighty empires and molded the early societies that have been left for us as a guide to past civilizations.

While the deities, heroes, and rulers described on these pages may prove only a legend to that guide, they may also provide the first step on an illuminating life-long journey into learning and understanding. After all, Rome wasn't the only great empire that was not built in a day . . . Greece and Egypt also took a while.

QUEEN MAKERI.

QUEEN MAKERI

 somewhat obscure figure of Egypt's 21st Dynasty, Queen Makeri is said to have been the daughter of a king of Tanis, which was located in the northern Delta region of the Nile.

From what research is available in reference to her, it is possible that she may have been a daughter of Pinudjem I, known by the name "Maatkare." This possible configuration of her name describes a woman who combined the roles of "God's Wife" and chief of the priestesses of Amun into one title—"Divine Adoratrice," which means "the sole wife of god."

Other sources list her as bearing the titles of "Divine Wife," "Royal Wife" and "Royal Mother."

Nonetheless, Egypt's 21st Dynasty—which ran from 1609 to 945 B.C.—initiated what historians have labeled as the Third Intermediate period. This era continued until 656 B.C., and included the 22nd, 23rd, 24th, and 25th dynasties. Also known as the time of the first Tanite Kings, the 21st Dynasty began when Smendes proclaimed himself king following the death of Rameses XI. This rule is noted as marking the end of the "renaissance" in Egypt, and it was during this period that many temples and other such large buildings were constructed and dedicated to a triad of gods, Amun, Mut, and Khonsu.

It is said that Makeri ventured south to marry King Pinezen I. She later died giving birth to a daughter, who did not survive her. Sources credit Makeri as the full regal heiress descendant of a long line of monarchs who wore the double-serpent crown.

QUEEN AAHMES

QUEEN AAHMES

A queen who ruled during the early years of Egypt's 18th Dynasty, Aahmes was the wife of Thothmes I (known in some sources as Tuthmosis I), who lived from 1504 to 1450 B.C.

Aahmes is listed as a daughter of Ahmose I and Ahmose-Nefertari, through other sources indicate she may have been the product of a union with a lesser-ranked wife—as was a popular custom among many of the ruling classes. Nonetheless, Aahmes is said to have been a half-sister of Amenhotep I, the father of her future husband, and it was Amenhotep I who gave his son her hand in marriage.

Though she is noted by some as a consort of the Egyptian god Amun, Queen Aahmes also bore a number of prestigious political and royal titles, including: "Divine Wife," "Great Royal Wife," "Royal Sister," and "Hereditary Princess."

Most of these were a result of her inheritance of full sovereign rights, passed to her by both of her parents, and through her subsequent wedding to Thothmes, the son of her half-brother, Amenhotep I. As such, it was also her marriage that helped the half-royal prince to attain the throne as King of Egypt. And though she held such prior rights to that throne, she yielded the task of governing the kingdom to him.

She later gave birth to four royal children, one of whom was Hatshepset, another 18th Dynasty ruler. Queen Aahmes died at a relatively young age and was buried at Thebes.

K. AMENOPHIS.

KING AMENOPHIS III

menophis III ruled from 1391 to 1353 B.C., at the height of the empire's 18th Dynasty—a time noted for great increases in Egypt's wealth, artistic growth, and exposure to a plethora of outside influences.

Amenophis III (who some sources cite as Amenhotep III), was born in Thebes, the son of Mutemwia, a concubine of Tuthmosis IV. He assumed the throne at the age of 12 and married during the second year of his reign, which may have been more of a political arrangement than the fruit of any romantic involvement.

Nonetheless, his wife—a woman of common descent named Tiye—bore him five daughters and two sons. While his first-born son died at an early age, his second son, Akenhaten, succeeded him to the throne as Amenophis IV. And though he later took many other wives, Tiye is known as the first to take advantage of her royal role as "the King's Great Wife," and later acted as a "queen mother." During her husband's rule, as well as during the early years of her son's, Queen Tiye is credited with overseeing matters of the growing empire's foreign policy.

Hailed as one of the greatest builders in the nation's history, Amenophis III is said to have covered the land with monuments. He is credited as the founder of many constructs, including the temple of Luxor and a temple to the goddess Mut.

Though his reign is primarily noted as a peaceful period, he is remembered, nonetheless, as a great warrior. He is celebrated as a chivalrous figure of the period, who delighted in the works that survived him. He died at the age of 55.

QUEEN AMENOPHIS

QUEEN
AMENOPHIS

ueen Amenophis was the "Great Royal Wife" of King Amenophis III, the ninth king of Egypt's 18th Dynasty. The couple's rule began around 1390 B.C., and though she is often associated with her husband's name, her original name was Tiye.

Despite a lack of royal birth, Queen Tiye is said to have exerted a great deal of influence over her husband and their son, Akhenaten (Amenophis IV). Their first-born, Thutmose, died at a young age and thus did not inherit the throne. The queen also bore numerous royal daughters, including the princesses Ast, Baketamon, Hentaneb, Hentmerheb, and Sitamun. The royal family lived in luxury and splendor at the palace of Malkata at Thebes, where it is said Queen Tiye was heavily involved with overseeing the scribes and other officials who handled the administrative aspects of governing the kingdom.

The couple's rule, and the subsequent reign of their son, is noted as a peaceful and prosperous time for the empire, which extended at that time from the region of the northern Sudan to the banks of the Euphrates River.

A daughter of Juas and Tuaa—and reportedly of Asiatic origin—Tiye was said to have been of fair complexion and blue-eyed. She is also noted as being among the most beautiful of all women depicted on the great monuments, which is supported by the fact that she is represented in sculptures, reliefs, and inscriptions to a greater degree than was customary.

K.RAMESES.III.

KING
RAMESES III

With his reign spanning from 1186 to 1154 B.C., Rameses III was the second ruler of Egypt's 20th Dynasty, following his father, Setnakhte, and his mother, Queen Tiye-merenese.

Rameses III is well-known as the last great warrior of Egypt—though his campaigns were typically defensive ones. His first conflict is listed as being with a coalition of Libyans, who were soundly routed and taken captive to labor in Egypt. Later, a northern invasion force was also successfully countered, as was a subsequent second effort by Libya. Rameses III also engaged in several campaigns against the Hittites and Syrians. However, after more than a decade of warfare under his rule, a period of peace was finally attained.

In addition to his prowess on the field of battle, Rameses III's reign over Egypt is also marked by prosperity and cultural enrichment—verified by his architectural accomplishments and the splendor of his tomb in the Valley of the Kings at Thebes. However, despite such lavish burial accommodations, his mummy was later discovered among a cache of royal corpses at Deir el-Bahri, which had been abandoned there by tomb robbers.

Rameses III's great queen was Ese. With her and his harem of many other wives, he is said to have had some 18 sons and 14 daughters. One of his sons, Rameses IV, eventually succeeded him in ruling the empire. However, his harem was said to have been the source of many scandals and other problems for the ruler—including an unsuccessful assassination attempt spawned with the alleged involvement of his second wife, Tiy.

Q.AMENARTAS

QUEEN
AMENARTAS

iewed as a minor figure of Egypt's 25th Dynasty, Queen Amenartas is often described as a "Royal Wife, Sister, and Daughter," as well as "Chief Prophetess" and "Divine Adoratrice."
The dynasty under which she ruled marked the beginning of what is known as the "Late Period" of Egypt's ancient history, which spanned from 747 to 525 B.C. Ironically, this Late Period would eventually lead to the end of Kushite rule by the family of Queen Amenartas. The period is also noted as preceding the first era of Persian rule of Egypt.

Amenartas, who is also known in other texts as Amenirdis, was a daughter of King Kashta—a Kushite who assumed rule of the Napatan throne around 760 B.C. Sources indicate he is likely to have also subsequently conquered Lower Nubia before expanding his rule over other areas of Egypt. Two of King Kashta's several children—Piankhy and Shabaka—succeeded him to the throne, and their sister, Amenartas, shared the crown with her two brothers in succession.

Some sources indicate that she held no greater importance than the co-regents with whom she was associated. However, she is credited by others with establishing Nubian control over Karnak through inheritance of important territories ruled by Osorkon III. This no doubt helped her brother Piankhy cement a role he later earned, through a series of military campaigns, as a unifier of Egypt, while Amenartas I assumed joint leadership of the priesthood of Amun.

Q·HATSHEPSET.

QUEEN HATSHEPSET

The heiress daughter of King Thothmes I and Queen Aahmes, Queen Hatshepset was the fifth ruler of Egypt's 18th Dynasty, reigning from 1473 to 1458 B.C. Hatshepset married her half-brother, Thothmes II, who died in 1479 B.C. Upon his death, his heir (who he had produced through a union with a concubine named Isis), Thothmes III, was still too young to rule alone. So Hatshepset ruled jointly with him until she later proclaimed herself as sole pharaoh.

Her self-declaration is said to have earned great support from the high priests and other court officials. However, there is some question about her appearance as a result of this bold move. While some say Hatshepset was a radiant beauty, others indicate that she may have preferred to adorn herself in more masculine attire and had herself depicted in sculptures and reliefs wearing all the garments of a male king—even a fake beard. The latter is more likely, given the aforementioned accounts of her assumption of the role of sole pharaoh—complete with all of its masculine offices and male vestiges.

Despite her clothing preferences, though, Hatshepset's reign was marked by maintenance of the empire's security and a number of building projects. She is credited with initiating construction on her famous temple at Deir el-Bahri, located on the western shore of the Nile at Thebes.

Hatshepset disappeared during a revolt in 1458 B.C. Afterward, her images were mutilated by her stepson's allies.

K.SETI. I

KING SETI I

King Seti I—the second king of Egypt's 19th Dynasty—was the son of Rameses I and Queen Sitre. His prosperous rule of the kingdom spanned from 1306 to 1290 B.C., and he produced a heir to the throne who was named Rameses II.

It is said that the Egyptians perceived the dawn of the new ruling family as a new beginning for the empire on the heels of the troubled period of the late 18th Dynasty.

Like his sire, Seti I (also known as Sethos I in some texts) was also known as a prominent military leader. Having set a goal of restoring the vast empire created by the Thuthmossid kings a century earlier, Seti I is credited with plundering Palestine, returning Damascus to Egyptian control, and reaching an accord with the Hittites. He also led a campaign into Kadesh. Many of his military exploits were depicted on the walls of the temple at Karnak, where he completed a major construction plan initiated by his father. During the project, Seti I coruled with his own son.

It is theorized that Seti I was likely wed to his queen, Tuya, prior to his becoming prince of the realm. In addition to Rameses II, she was also the mother of his two daughters, Tia and Hentmire.

Seti I's vast tomb is located in the Valley of the Kings at Thebes. It is the largest in the area—cut some 300 feet into the face of sheer cliffs, it boasts a myriad of passageways and elaborate, ornate chambers with vaulted ceilings. However, this location was later said to have been vandalized by tomb robbers, and Seti I's body was relocated to Deir el-Bahri.

Q.CLEOPATRA

QUEEN CLEOPATRA

There is probably no Egyptian ruler that has been romanticized as much as Queen Cleopatra. Known more precisely as Cleopatra VII, she still reigns today in a way, along with the popular boy-king Tutankhamen (King Tut), as the most well-known of Egypt's ancient rulers. And though she was not born until 69 B.C., her story may more aptly begin around 332 B.C.—when Egypt was added to the empire of Macedonian conqueror Alexander the Great. Following Alexander's death 10 years later, a general in his army named Ptolemy became king. And it was from Ptolemy I that Cleopatra descended, ruling as a member of the Ptolemaic Dynasty.

She began her reign at the age of 17 and later spent a period of time living with Julius Caesar. It was later that she began what has become an often fictionalized relationship (both a marriage and a political alliance) with Roman coruler Mark Anthony, who was dueling for power in Rome with Octavian. Cleopatra's alleged entanglement with Mark Anthony led his rival to declare war on Egypt, resulting in the country becoming a Roman province in 30 B.C.

That was also the same year Cleopatra died, at the age of 39. Though it was likely inevitable—as Octavian reportedly had no interest in negotiating with the fallen Egyptian queen—her death is believed to have been self-inflicted with the help of a venomous asp. With the Roman conquest of the once mighty empire, Cleopatra is known as Egypt's "Last Pharaoh."

P.NEFERT.

PRINCESS NEFERT

A queen during Egypt's 12th Dynasty, Princess Nefert was a consort of Ammenemes I, who began his rule in 1991 B.C. Nerfert—known in some texts as Neferu—is said to have been a hereditary princess of a royal clan. This is substantiated by research into a possible connection between her lineage and the house of Snofru, who founded Egypt's Fourth Dynasty around 2625 B.C.

Nefert is also often associated with such prestigious titles as: "the Hereditary Princess," "the Great Favorite," "the Beloved Consort of the King," and "the Ruler of All Women."

Such heritage surrounding her is said to have proven quite useful to Ammenemes I, who was not of royal blood. A commoner of Nubian descent, he seized the throne upon the death of the last 11th Dynasty king, Mentuhotpe IV, for whom he served as a vizier. It is thus assumed that Ammenemes I married Nefert out of political motives to strengthen his claim to the throne, which marked the beginning of the 12th Dynasty. If this was indeed the case, some historians conclude that she must have been a woman of considerable wealth and power, which would have been needed to provide a usurper of common ancestry with sufficient prestige to take the throne.

Described by Egyptologists as "a good and beautiful woman," Nefert is believed to have died very young—around the age of 24 or 25. She is said to have been buried in a small pyramid located near the tomb of the king.

Q.ARSINOE.II

QUEEN ARSINOE II

A crown princess of Thrace, Queen Arsinoe II was the wife of King Ptolemy II, also known as Philadelphus.

The Ptolemies' reign followed the conquest of Egypt by the Macedonian conqueror Alexander the Great around the end of the 300th century B.C.—which many sources note as sounding the death knell to the kingdom's longstanding political autonomy.

Following the death of Alexander and that of Philip Arrhidaeus and Alexander IV, the two subsequent kings who comprised the Macedonian Dynasty—Ptolemy I, who had been a general in Alexander's army, became Egypt's king in 304 B.C. This marked the onset of what was known as the Ptolemaic period, which continued until 30 B.C., when a much celebrated descendant of this line, Cleopatra, ultimately lost the kingdom to the Roman Octavian. Egypt remained under the Roman Empire's rule until the sixth century A.D., when the country was conquered by Arab Muslims who converted the Egyptians to Islam.

Nonetheless, in the period of Ptolemaic rule nearly a millenium earlier, Queen Arsinoe II was elevated to the role of a great figure in the Egyptian world. She bore her husband three children and is also said to have adopted the son of her disgraced rival. Queen Arsinoe II was also honored with many fine statues in her likeness in other parts of the world, such as Athens, Greece. Following her death, even more honors were bestowed posthumously upon Queen Arsinoe II by her grieving husband throughout the remaining years of his reign.

K. THOTHMES. III

KING THOTHMES III

hough he was not of royal descent, Thothmes III is described by some sources as "the Alexander the Great of ancient Egypt." He reportedly earned this title by conquering the known world of his day and carving the names of more than 600 fallen nations and captured cities on the walls of Karnak. However, at home—under the rule of a powerful and ambitious stepmother—his rise to power proves to have been somewhat less meteoric.

It seems Thothmes III did not assume control of his kingdom until his late father's wife, Queen Hatshepset, died in 1458 B.C. Though she had ruled jointly with him during his youth, Queen Hatshepset's ire at the child's birth by a concubine of her late husband, Thothmes II, subsequently led her to assume the role of sole pharaoh. The move was bolstered by her unquestionable royal lineage and support of the royal court. As a result, Thothmes III was left to toil in relative insignificance. However, he is said to have spent his time training with the Egyptian army, where he fueled the fires of his hatred for his stepmother, who kept him from the throne for so long. The experience he gained there no doubt contributed to his military skill and strategic prowess, which ultimately earned him remembrance as a world conqueror.

Domestically, "Egypt's greatest pharaoh" also excelled at construction, as befit a good ruler. Following another ruling tradition, he also had several wives—including Neferu, a child of his father and stepmother.

Thothmes III was buried in a tomb in the Valley of the Kings, leaving the kingdom to his heir, Amenophis II.

DIANA.

DIANA

iana is primarily known as the goddess of the hunt—though it is also said that an aversion to marriage earned her additional duty as a protectress of virgins.

To the Greeks, Diana was known as Artemis, and those legends indicate that, along with her twin brother, Apollo, she was born of a union between Leto and Zeus. When Hera, Zeus' wife, learned of the impending birth, Leto was cursed to deliver her illegitimate offspring in utter darkness. The Greek name "Artemis" probably meant "bright one," leading to her affiliation with the moon.

For this reason, Diana is also called Luna by the Romans.

In Greek mythology, Artemis is also said to have aided her mother in her brother's delivery, which came nine days later. This substantiates another of her roles—goddess of childbirth. Her guardianship of virginity and chastity is said to have been cemented in her response to Actaeon when she caught him watching her bathe. She turned the voyeur into a deer that was subsequently torn to pieces by his own dogs.

But the primary role of Diana, or Artemis, is that of huntress. And while it is said that she engaged in the hunt at a very early age, her portrayal of this persona may best be seen in her close friendship with perhaps mythology's most prominent hunter, Orion. For, as legend has it, Orion earned his celestial prominence as a constellation when Artemis set his image in the heavens after Apollo tricked her into slaying him out of jealousy of their friendship.

JUPITER.

JUPITER

upiter was considered by the Romans to be the father of all gods and men, and it was believed that souls were emanations from him, to whom they returned after death. He is generally depicted seated upon a throne of gold or ivory, bearing deadly lightning bolts in his mighty hands.

It would take nearly an entire book in itself to detail the mythological genealogy of Jupiter's origin and all the children with whom he is associated. Simply put, however, you could say his story is "like father, like son."

Jupiter—or Zeus in Greek mythology—is the youngest child of Cronus, who was the youngest of the Titans, a generation of giant godlike beings born of Uranus (the sky) and Gaia (the earth). After Cronus overthrew his father as King of the Gods, he was warned by an oracle that one of his own children would do the same to him. So, in an attempt to thwart the dreaded prophecy of doom, Cronus devoured each of his children at birth.

When Zeus was born, however, his mother, Rhea, tricked her husband into sparing the child by wrapping a stone in baby clothing, which Cronus consumed. Rhea also caused Cronus to regurgitate her other children. After growing to adulthood in secrecy on Crete, Zeus returned to lead his elder siblings in a rebellion against their father—fulfilling the prophecy and forging the third generation of gods, the Olympians.

MARS

MARS

Mars is perhaps best known as the Roman god of war. Known to the Greeks as Ares, one of the 12 ruling Olympians, he is described as possessing an unrivaled passion for the savage and noble arts of war.

Mars thrived on the thrill of conflict and did whatever he could to incite it. It must also be noted, though, that even though he loved the clash of warriors' weapons, he was not a good strategist and often wound up on the losing side. In fact, it is said that having the war god on your side offered no great promise of a victory. For example, in Greek mythology Ares supported the Trojans in their unsuccessful war against the Greeks. However, Hades, the Greek god of the dead, is said to have appreciated the war god for the supply of new souls his battles provided.

Due to his bellicose nature, Mars holds an esteemed position in the Roman pantheon of gods and deities. And to the Romans, this only son of Jupiter and Juno was also the god of shepherds and seers. And though he is said to have remained a bachelor, he is cited as the father of a number of children born to goddess and mortal alike—two of which were Romulus and Remus, who are credited with founding Rome in 753 B.C. In the Greek myths, one of Ares' most flagrant affairs was with the irresistible Aphrodite, even though she was married to another.

Mars often traveled in bad company. His sister, Bellona (Eris, the goddess of discord in the Greek myths), was the Roman goddess of war and cruelty. In the Greek legends, the names of his Ares' twin sons—Deimus and Phobus— meant "panic" and "fear."

BACCHUS

BACCHUS

acchus is perhaps the one deity to whom mere mortals are most indebted. After all, he is best known as the god of wine. Often accompanied by Centaurs, Satyrs, and Maenads, Bacchus is said to have traveled the countrysides of Europe and Asia teaching the art of grape cultivation and fermentation, as well as many other fine elements of human civilization.

His labors also elevated him to the status of being one of the 12 ruling Olympians in Greek mythology. Known as Dionysus among those Greek myths, Bacchus was the son of Zeus and Semele, a mortal.

According to the Greek legend, Hera (Zeus's wife) tricked Semele into enraging Zeus, prompting the King of Heaven to slay her with one of his dreaded lightning bolts. The story goes that Hermes rescued the unborn fetus Dionysus and sewed him inside Zeus' leg, and he later delivered the child at full term. But Hera was undaunted in her anger, and ordered the Titans to rip the child to pieces and boil the remains. Dionysus's grandmother, Rhea, intervened and reanimated the infant, who was subsequently raised as a girl to avoid further retaliation from Hera. But, alas, even long, effeminate locks failed to dissuade Hera from later discovering the youth's true identity. Thus Zeus was forced to have Hermes change Dionysus into a ram and hide him in a cave to protect him from the wrath of his angry and jealous wife. But Hera eventually found him there, too, and finally drove him to insanity—but not before he had invented the succulent elixir for which he is known: wine.

PAN

42 ש EGYPTIAN KINGS AND QUEENS AND CLASSICAL DEITIES

PAN

nimal horns protruding from atop his human-looking head and cloven hooves instead of feet mark Pan as the chief god of shepherds and their flocks. His dominion was forests, hills, and green pastures. Known for his fabled musical pipes—on which he was quite skilled—he is also represented as being fond of dancing with the nymphs of the wood.

A Greek divinity, Pan was known to the Romans as Faunus. His unique half-man, half-goat physique led his mother to abandon him—so Hermes delivered him to Mount Olympus, where he served as amusement for the gods. Centuries later, the image of Pan was adapted as one of the various portrayals of Satan in the Christian mythology that followed.

Pan is attributed as being playful and prone to the more riotous effects of strong drink. He was also a boastful partaker of the pleasures of the opposite sex, claiming to have chased and caught a considerable host of mortal and not-so-mortal women and nymphs—or at least he tried.

In one such instance, while attempting to romance a chaste woman named Syrinx, she ran to the River Ladon and turned herself into a reed to escape the goat-man's advances. When Pan could not distinguish his quarry from the other reeds, he cut several reeds into varying lengths and strung them together, creating the crude musical instrument that still bears his name in the modern age, panpipes.

Pan was also believed to have been able to inspire sudden fear in groups of people for no apparent reason—thus the origin of the word "panic."

JUNO

JUNO

uno—the highest and most powerful divinity next to her husband, Jupiter—was the daughter of Saturn and Rhea.

To the Greeks, she was known as Hera and was worshiped as the goddess of women. Her domain as a deity was over marriage and the lives of women in general.

Like her powerful brothers, Juno was also swallowed at birth by her father (Cronus, in the Greek myths). This was done because of his fear of a prophecy that one of his own children would depose him as King of the Gods, as he had done to his own father. Fortunately, her mother, Rhea, caused Cronus to regurgitate Juno and her brothers, and they joined Jupiter in overthrowing the Titans.

The celebration of Juno's wedding to Jupiter (Zeus in the Greek myths) turned out to be a tremendous occasion, fostening a plethora of myths and stories in its own right. Their honeymoon is said to have lasted 300 years—though Jupiter later proved to be an unfaithful husband. While Juno is known as the mother of Mars and Vulcan—the gods of war and of blacksmiths, respectively—it was the many illegitimate children her husband fathered that kept her occupied in her role as a jealous wife. Juno appears in various legends trying to gain vengance against the semi-divine children of Jupiter, such as Hercules.

However, she also found time to endeavor in prophesy and grant such power to others. Hera also played a pivotal role in aiding the Greeks during the Trojan war.

NEPTUNE.

NEPTUNE

eptune—or Poseidon, as he was known to the Greeks—is the undisputed ruler of all of watery realms, not only the seas. He was the son of Saturn, the brother of Jupiter (Zeus), and the husband of Amphitrite.

Most legends attribute his connection to the sea as the luck of the draw. In the Greek myths, Poseidon was a son of Cronus (known as Saturn to the Romans), who devoured his children at his birth so that none would grow to usurp his throne. Some myths say Poseidon's mother, Rhea, tricked Cronus into eating a young horse instead—as she spared her other son, Zeus, by replacing him with a stone. However, others relate that Rhea caused Cronus to regurgitate the children he had swallowed, and thus Poseidon was released. Zeus then led a rebellion against Cronus, along with Poseidon and their other brother, Hades, which ended in their father's defeat. The three then cast lots for control of the world's realms, with Zeus becoming the supreme ruler of the Olympian gods, Hades assuming dominion of the underworld and the spirits of the dead, and Poseidon claiming rule over all sources of water.

The symbol of his power was a three-pronged spear, called a trident. With it, he could call forth or quell the ocean's storms. Other icons related to him were the dolphin and the horse. Neptune is credited not only with creating the horse, but also with teaching mortals the use of bit and bridle to ride the creatures. Like his brothers and most of the gods, Neptune enjoyed meddling in the affairs of mortals, and often used his powers to affect the tides of wars as well as those of the ocean.

CLYTIE

CLYTIE

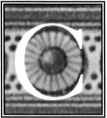lytie's claim to fame is linked to her presence among the long line of women with whom Apollo, the Sun God, became enamored.

A daughter of two titans, Oceanus and Tethys, Clytie evidently shared the sun god's infatuation, and for a while the couple enjoyed a romantic relationship. Until, that is, Apollo happened upon another woman—an Assyrian princess named Leucothoe.

Apollo then disguised himself as a woman and went off to pursue his newfound obsession, abandoning poor Clytie. She became so enraged at his rejection of her affections that she devised a plan to avenge herself upon her former lover. She exposed Apollo's activities to Leucothoe's father, who was equally enraged. However, since he could do little against an Olympian, he opted to take his anger out on his disobedient child instead. The angry father disciplined his daughter by having her buried alive.

Distraught at his lover's fate, Apollo sprinkled nectar on the site of the burial, which caused a new kind of tree to grow upon the site. This tree is known as frankincense, named for the aromatic gum resin it "weeps."

Crushed by his compassion for her romantic rival, Clytie sat and fasted for more than a week, until she eventually sprouted roots and turned into a sunflower. And to this day, her mournful stare at Apollo as he crosses the daytime sky is said to be the reason the sunflower turns its face toward the sun.

MINERVA

MINERVA

inerva is known in Greek mythology as Athene. In both incarnations, she is known as the goddess of wisdom, arts, and sciences, and is credited with inventing the flute and trumpet.

Minerva is also considered the goddess of the so-called "womanly arts"—cooking, spinning, and weaving—and is also known as protectress of agriculture. In this aspect, she is hailed as inventor of the plow, rake, yoke, and various other implements used in the tasks of planting and harvesting. On her fiercer side, she was also the goddess of war and determined the fates of individuals in battle.

In that aspect, she is often known as Pallas, after a friend she accidentally killed with a spear while sparring. Minerva was quite active on the side of the Greeks during the Trojan war.

A cloud of obscurity hovers around her legendary origin—particularly before the source of her paternal lineage. In different stories, Zeus, Poseidon, and Itonus, a titan, are each credited as being her father. One version is that Zeus was enamored by a mortal woman and had his way with her against her will. When a prophecy decreed that a girl would be born—but any subsequent sons born to the woman would grow to avenge the wrong done by Zeus—the deity devoured the woman. Later, however, Zeus developed a crushing headache that was so painful, he asked one of the other gods to open his skull with a sharp axe. From that wound sprang Minerva, fully grown and wearing armor.

MERCURY.

MERCURY

nown as Hermes in the Greek myths, Mercury was the son of Jupiter (Zeus) and Maia, one of the daughters of Atlas. He was said to have been born in a cave on Mount Cyllene in Arcadia. But he apparently wasted little time in creating a place for himself in the Olympian family, alongside whom he fought against the giants.

Though some legends portray him as little more than a messenger for the gods, other accounts indicate he was quite a busy enforcer of the will of Jupiter. As the herald of the gods, Mercury is said to have been responsible for the safety of the other gods. Adorned with his staff and winged sandals, he was also well known as the god of eloquence for his speaking skills. Yet others looked upon him as the god of roads, who protected travelers. As a Roman divinity, he was the patron of commerce and gain, as well as the god of music and chemistry. Some have even gone as far as to attribute Mercury as a patron saint of thieves and a god of wealth.

Yet, he was not without his carnal side. In Greek mythology, Hermes is said to have had a romantic rendezvous with Aphrodite, which was a "reward" for his role in convincing the other gods to spare her from punishment when she was caught in an adulterous situation with Ares (Mars) by her husband. However, the product of their one-time tryst was Hermaphroditus, a double-sexed being.

Mercury is the name given to the planet closest to the sun in the earth's solar system.

AJAX

Known as "Great Ajax," this mortal warrior was born in Salamis, the son of Telamon and Periboea. He put little stock in the meddling of the gods in human affairs and is often described as arrogant, self-absorbed, and having a problem with authority. However, in terms of courage and bravery, Ajax is said to have surpassed all but Achilles—with whom he fought the heroes of the city of Troy.

Ajax's body was said to be impervious to steel, which tipped the points of arrows in the Trojan war. This handy attribute is credited to Hercules, who covered the newborn Ajax with his invulnerable lion's pelt, and the properties of the pelt applied to the infant. When Achilles was slain, it was Ajax who defended his fallen comrade's corpse, carrying it to safety through enemy lines with help from brave Odysseus. However, as heroic as Ajax's deed was, it later sparked a conflict that would eventually lead to his demise.

Ajax engaged in a competition with Odysseus and Menelaus for Achilles' enchanted armor. And when Agamemmnon awarded the prize to his rivals, Ajax sought revenge. However, thanks to a little divine intervention by Athene, Ajax was tricked and later opted to slay himself. He tried to take his own life, throwing himself onto his own sword, but his tough skin caused the weapon to bend and it failed to penetrate. A subsequent attempt was successful, though, after Ajax discovered his armpit was the one place he could be wounded.

Due to the manner of his death, great Ajax was denied a noble cremation on a warrior's pyre, and was buried in a coffin at Cape Rhoeteum. Some say Odysseus later lost Achilles' prized armor from his ship on his way home and it washed ashore at the very spot where Ajax was buried.

VENUS

VENUS

alled Aphrodite (which means "sea foam") by the Greeks, Venus has been a popular subject of artists in virtually all mediums throughout the ages. She is held as the highest ideal of female beauty and love.

Also known as the goddess of desire, legend has it Venus was conceived and arose from the foam of the surf at Cythera after Cronus threw Uranus into the sea. Grass and flowers sprang forth wherever her bare feet touched the earth, and the seasons served as her clothing. Some attribute the legend of her watery birth to the reported aphrodisiac qualities of seafood.

Given her typical state of attire, it's not surprising that Venus was adopted by Jupiter (Zeus). The goddess' sole duty as a deity was engaging in and promoting love—a tough job, but evidently someone had to do it. But her charms and attention were often as much a curse as a blessing. Though she was desired by all and had her choice of partners, she wed Hephaestus (Vulcan), a craftsman, according to the Greek legend, and became known as the patroness of mechanical arts. However, her three children were fathered by Mars (Ares in the Greek legend), the god of war—an adultery that eventually became more than the craftsman could bear.

Hephaestus ensnared the devious couple and told the other gods about their misdeeds. Although the Olympians refused to pass judgment at the time because of Venus's beauty, she was later punished by Jupiter.

ANDROMEDA

ANDROMEDA

hough primarily a tale of mortals, the romantic story of Andromeda remains to this day one of the more "stellar" myths of the Romans.

Andromeda was the daughter of King Cepheus of Ethiopia and his queen, Cassiopeia, who boasted that she and her offspring were even more desirable than the Nereids. This assessment of the 50 sea-nymphs, or mermaids, angered Neptune. His ire caused the sea god to seek vengeance by summoning a mammoth sea monster, the Kracken, to destroy Philistia, the country's capital. However, an oracle told Cepheus the city would be spared if Andromeda were to be sacrificed to the creature. Thus he had her chained to an outcropping of rock overlooking the coast, as an offering to the beast to save the kingdom.

Enter the hero, Perseus, who rescued Andromeda with a little help from the severed head of Medusa, whom he had killed during his adventures. Medusa was a woman who had snakes for hair, and she could turn anyone who looked at her face to stone. When the Kracken neared the rocks where Andromeda was chained, Perseus lifted the head of Medusa and turned the monster into a stone statue, which quickly sank beneath the waves.

The rescue, as well as Andromeda's desire for an immediate wedding to Perseus, sparked a battle that pitted him against her parents and her betrothed, Phineus. During the conflict, Perseus once again used Medusa's head as a weapon, and he emerged victorious, taking Andromeda as his wife.

Later, Andromeda, Cassiopeia, Cepheus, and Perseus were placed among the stars in the heavens by Athene. Today, you can still see their constellations after nightfall in the northern hemisphere. Look in the vicinity of Polaris, the north star.

A CHRONOLOGY OF ANCIENT EGYPT

3150–2700 B.C. Thinite Period (Dynasties 1–2)

2700–2200 B.C. Old Kingdom (Dynasties 3–6)

2200–2040 B.C. First Intermediate Period (Dynasties 7–11)

2040–1674 B.C. Middle Kingdom (Dynasties 11–14)

1674–1553 B.C. Second Intermediate Period (Dynasties 14–17)

1553–1069 B.C. New Kingdom (Dynasties 18–20)

1069–702 B.C. Third Intermediate Period (Dynasties 21–23)

747–525 B.C. Late Period (Dynasties 24–26)

525–404 B.C. First Persian Period (Dynasty 27)

404–399 B.C. Dynasties 28–30

343–332 B.C. Second Persian Period

332 B.C.–395 A.D. Greco-Roman Period (includes Ptolemaic Period, from 304 B.C.–30 B.C.)

A Chronology of Greek and Roman Civilization

2,000-1,000 B.C. - Greek civilization begins to emerge in the region from the Caspian Sea to the eastern Mediterranean Sea. Near the end of the millenium, around 1193 B.C., the city of Troy is believed to have fallen to the Greeks.

900-700 B.C. - It was during this period that Homer is credited with creating the *Iliad* and *Odyssey*—epic poetic tales of the Greek heroes, gods, and goddesses, during and after the Trojan War. Also during this era, another Greek poet, Hesiod, wrote *Theogony*, which describes the origins of the Greek gods.

700-600 B.C. - The first recorded Greek Olympic games occurred during this century. In Italy, the city of Rome was founded in 753 B.C.

500-300 B.C. - Temples to Apollo and Zeus are erected at Corinth and Athens. In Rome, a temple is constructed for Saturn. In 390 B.C., Gauls from northern Italy sack the city of Rome, which is later rebuilt.

300-150 B.C. - The Roman republic grows stronger with victory over a rival city, Carthage, in the Punic Wars.

150-1 B.C. - The Romans continue to extend their power, and Greece, Gaul (France), and Britain come under Roman control during this period. After the murder of Julius Caesar in 44 B.C., his nephew Octavian, later known as Caesar Augustus, becomes the first Roman emperor. The 200 years following his rule, the *Pax Romana,* were a time of great prosperity for Rome.

476 A.D. - Fall of the Roman Empire.

INDEX ✿

FURTHER READING

Bierlein, J.F. *Parallel Myths.* New York: Ballentine Books, 1994.

Bunson, Margaret. *The Encyclopedia of Ancient Egypt.* New York: Facts On File Inc., 1991.

David, Rosalie and Anthony E. *A Biographical Dictionary of Ancient Egypt.* London: B.A. Seaby Ltd., 1992.

Flaum, Eric. *The Encyclopedia of Mythology: Gods, Heroes and Legends of the Greeks and Romans.* New York: Michael Friedman Publishing Group Inc., 1993.

Grimal, Nicolas. *A History of Ancient Egypt.* Oxford, U.K. and Cambridge, Mass.: Blackwell Publishers, 1992.

Macrone, Michael. *By Jove! Brush Up Your Mythology.* London: Pavillion Books Ltd., 1993.

Strouhal, Eugen. *Life of the Ancient Egyptians.* Norman: University of Oklahoma Press (by special arrangement with OPUS Publishing Ltd., London), 1992.

Vandenberg, Philipp. *The Golden Pharaoh.* New York: MacMillan Publishing Co. Inc., 1980.

Vercoutter, Jean. *The Search For Ancient Egypt.* New York: Harry N. Abrams Inc., 1992.